State of New York Legislature

Proceedings of the Senate of the State of New York

On the Death of Hon. Henry R. Low

State of New York Legislature

Proceedings of the Senate of the State of New York
On the Death of Hon. Henry R. Low

ISBN/EAN: 9783337160845

Printed in Europe, USA, Canada, Australia, Japan

Cover: Foto ©Suzi / pixelio.de

More available books at **www.hansebooks.com**

In Memoriam.

———

Henry R. Low.

———

"In halls of State he stood for many years.
Like fabled knight. his visage all aglow,
Receiving, giving sternly, blow for blow ;
Champion of right."

PROCEEDINGS

OF THE

S E N A T E

OF THE

State of New York,

ON THE DEATH OF

Hon. HENRY R. LOW.

———

ALBANY:
THE TROY PRESS COMPANY, PRINTERS.
1889.

PROCEEDINGS

OF THE

SENATE OF THE STATE OF NEW YORK,

ON THE DEATH OF

Hon. Henry R. Low.

IN SENATE.

JANUARY 1, 1889.

Mr. VEDDER offered the following :

WHEREAS, On the occasion of its convening to-day
the Senate is deprived by death of the presence of one
of its members, the late HENRY R. Low, the representative of the Thirteenth district, who died in the city of
New York on the first day of December last; and

WHEREAS, His long and distinguished career,
especially as a member of this body, calls for honorable recognition by his colleagues; be it, therefore,

Resolved, That a committee of five be appointed by
the President of the Senate to prepare resolutions commemorative of the character and services of our late
associate, and that Thursday, the seventeenth instant,

B

be designated as the day for receiving and acting upon the resolutions thus to be prepared and submitted for the consideration of the Senate.

The PRESIDENT put the question whether the Senate would agree to said resolution, and it was decided in the affirmative.

The PRESIDENT appointed as such committee Messrs. VEDDER, SLOAN, ERWIN, McNAUGHTON and PIERCE.

IN SENATE.

JANUARY 16, 1889.

Mr. VEDDER, from the special committee appointed to prepare resolutions in reference to the death of the Hon. HENRY R. LOW, asked that the time for presenting said resolutions be extended until Monday evening, February fourth.

The PRESIDENT put the question whether the Senate would agree to said request, and it was decided in the affirmative.

In Memoriam.

FEBRUARY 4, 1889.

Mr. VEDDER, from the select committee appointed to prepare resolutions commemorative of the character and services of Hon. HENRY R. LOW, late Senator, offered the following:

WHEREAS, The Hon. HENRY R. Low, a Senator of this State, and President *pro tempore* of this body, died in the city of New York, on the 1st day of December, 1888; be it, therefore,

Resolved, That holding his memory in affectionate regard, we mourn his untimely death.

Resolved, That in the office of Senator he exhibited the highest gifts of statesmanship, the loftiest patriotism and the most stainless integrity, and that in his death the State has lost a faithful servant, liberty an advocate and humanity a friend.

Resolved, That his private life was as pure and gentle as his public career was noble and distinguished, and that we tender to his family the sympathy which flows from hearts which are deeply moved with a great sorrow.

Resolved, That these resolutions be engrossed, and a copy thereof be presented to his children.

Senator SLOAN spoke as follows:

Mr. PRESIDENT: It sometimes happens in our experiences that we listen to tributes to departed

7

friends so laudatory as to be manifestly over-
wrought. Such tributes are not grateful because
unreal. They fail to hold the mirror up to nature.
While the omission of some defect of character
may well be pardoned at such a time, violations
of truth can not be. But when a career is ended
of which it can be said that it epitomized faithful
public service, good citizenship, loyal friendships,
kind intercourse with neighbors, devoted head-
ship to the family, we say, in truth, that a great
loss has been sustained. Such, I believe, without
coloring, was the career of our late associate.

Only as a Senator can I speak from personal
knowledge of Senator Low, but the testimony of
friends, the tributes everywhere heard in the
community where he lived, so abundantly attest
his sympathy with the public welfare, as also the
possession of exemplary traits of character, that
there is no need for me to speak in praise, except
as I knew him in our relations as members of this
body. It may well be left to the city of Middle-
town to proclaim his enterprise and public spirit.
I am told that there are few business organiza-
tions, industrial in their character, originating in
combined effort in that city, with which our
friend was not at some stage of their existence
in greater or less degree identified. He was in
the front always as a benefactor of his city, as he

was also in the front as an indefatigable worker
for the district he represented in this body. So,
too, was he an able, industrious and aggressive
advocate of all that he believed to be advanta-
geous to the State. Senator Low was a man whose
evolution of subjects brought out pronounced
convictions. His convictions were not the reflex
of the opinions of others. They were emphat-
ically his own, and he had the courage of his
convictions.

We all know of his persistence in contending
for the adoption of measures which he espoused
during the years of his service here. I think it
may be said that no Senator was more watchful
of general legislation. Apparently he was impressed with the responsibility which long
service imposes. Therefore, his voice was never
silent when he thought it ought to be heard.

Senator Low was, in one respect, the most
remarkable man I ever knew. I do not recall
another legislator of my acquaintance who, when
burdened with so many responsibilities as to be
really overburdened, was willing to take on new
ones, as Senator Low was always ready to.

Many times he has talked with me in committee, and elsewhere, about the possibility of
formulating new policies, when I knew that he
had more work to perform than from my point

of view it was possible to compass; and yet he would be interested and eager to lend the assistance of his advocacy to any new measure, or to make his influence felt in opposition, as the opinions he entertained might dictate.

Literally he seemed never to have enough to do, and yet with all of his cares, under the pressure of responsibilities grave and urgent, he was ever the courteous gentleman, lending his ear and counsel, as if his mind were as free as the air we breathe, to help in the attainment of ends which his judgment approved.

In this regard he was extraordinary, if I may not say, indeed, that he was a unique personality. To the possession of this quality of even temper, united with determination and vigor, it is not too much to say, the State is indebted for some of its most benefincet legislation.

Especially was Senator Low's advocacy valuable in the enactment of laws to protect the agricultural and dairy interests of the State. I think I do not state the case too strongly when I say that the dairymen of the State of New York look upon the death of Senator Low as an irreparable loss.

They had learned to lean upon him as their never-failing and never-hesitating champion. They recognize the fact that his advocacy of

their interests was always a potent influence in
their favor. They have a conviction that without
that advocacy their success in advancing measures of legislation would have been less assured
and, in all probability, less promptly realized. I
know from expressions of its members at a late
meeting of the State Association, what the pre-
vailing opinion is. The members of that association feel that a friend indeed has gone. They
feel that Senator Low's death is not only a
misfortune to them, but a misfortune to the
district he represented, as well as to the State
at large. These gentlemen were attached to
him, not only by ties of gratitude for the service rendered them, but they were his personal
friends, and they loved him for himself, apart
from other considerations.

Senator Low was indeed a lovable man ; not,
in the common acceptation of the term, a mag-
netic man, and yet he was a most agreeable com-
panion. He loved the society of his friends. He
found pleasure in elevating associations. In the
intercourse of those who gathered about him
he contributed intellectuality and cheer. His
knowledge was general, practical and accurate.
He told what he wanted to tell with cleverness
and force, and no one possessed keener appreciation of the refinements of humor than he.

Senator Low had not reached the age which would identify him with the gentlemen of the old school ; and yet, in some respects, he reflected that mold of manhood. His was not the temperament however, to incline one to be placed in that relation, because in our interpretation, a gentleman of the old school is more an observer than an actor in the drama of life. Senator Low was not the man to ever have reached a period of inactivity. Though he had lived to the allotted time of three-score years and ten, or even four-score years, I believe he would still have been found in the harness, unless restrained by disabling causes.

But for this pervading energy of his character, he might in the evening of life have settled into the typical old-school gentleman. I say this because of his native refinement, his culture, his courtesy, his generosity ; but notwithstanding the possession of these qualities, qualities implied by the soubriquet, the activity of his nature was a constant contradiction of such an ideality. It might be said of Senator Low that while he was a gentleman of the old school, he was yet a type of Americanism which knows no restraint ; a combination of energy and urbanity not quite common in the civilization of our day.

In Memoriam.

Although sixty-two years of age when he died, no one who knew Senator Low, at the close of the session of the last Senate, would have considered him other than a man in the maturity of active manhood.

When we parted company in this chamber, less than a year ago however — at the beginning of the season when the redolence of flowers and the songs of birds filled the air with gladness, a time when one would wish to live always — we saw, I think, that the form and features of our friend foretold his doom.

I know that something seemed to tell me that another spring-time would find the chair of the absent Senator empty. And so it is. Loving hands have placed flowers where he sat. We look at these flowers, these tokens of affection, these emblems of mortality, and while we look at them we recall only pleasant recollections of his presence.

If moistened eyes turn that way, tell me not that they turn in weakness. Tell me not that tears may be shed by women only. Tears may be shed by strong men when a brother falls, and they may be shed without confessing weakness, without dishonor. Senators, the death of one of our number comes very close to all of us, not only in sundering ties of brotherhood,

which grow out of our associations here,
but when the circle of thirty-three men
is broken even by the loss of one, it speaks
perforce a word we ought not to treat indif-
ferently. We know that "it is appointed unto
all men once to die," and yet death in itself is so
impenetrable a mystery that few of us care to
dwell upon its meaning. We know that it comes
nearer with each recurring day and hour. It is
well that we are buoyed with hope, that we can
contemplate death, and yet not realize in our
own personalities how near it may be, or that in
the light of human ken, every moment of our
lives, it is as near to us as it is to others. True,
we see that the flight of time is to all alike, and
not less marked by the sun than the daily less-
ening period of our existence is.

Also, true it is, that these flying years bring new
environments. Darker shadows cross our path.
We turn away from these shadows to live in the
fantasy of earlier days. But when we come back
to the realities about us, a grimmer humor veils
our eyes; speculation takes the place of fancy,
imagination sinks into philosophy, and

> "As life runs on, the road grows strange
>   With faces new, and near the end
> The mile-stones into head-stones change,
>   'Neath every one a friend."

In Memoriam.

Senator PIERCE spoke as follows:

Mr. PRESIDENT: The customary period of public mourning for eminent citizens who have served and adorned our State and country and passed away while in the exercise of important official functions, made appropriate by the decease of our colleague while holding the constitutional office of temporary president of the Senate, is about expiring. The drapery that for the past month has lain in solemn folds over his vacant desk and sadly festooned the chair of the President of the Senate, to symbolize the shadow cast, not only in this chamber, but over the State, when the angel of death, on his tireless wings, paused and hovered in his endless flight and fixed his fatal glance on our departed colleague, is now to be removed. These symbols have been the catafalque of HENRY R. LOW; they indicate that by public authority he was lying in solemn state in the principal chamber of the Capitol assigned for legislative deliberation. The distinction of being leader of the Senate (not new to him), was readily accorded to him by us when he returned to it after an absence of nearly twenty years, ripe in experience and rich in the wide reputation for probity and genius and public usefulness, acquired in projecting and carrying out enterprises, vast in their scope and grandly

15

beneficent in their conception and results. Twenty-six years ago, nineteen of which he was absent from the Senate, he was the acknowledged leader of the Senate and of his party, and chairman of the Republican State Committee. He thought and breathed a political atmosphere that was not altogether fragrant to me, but which gave such vigor to him, then scarcely thirty-seven years of age, as led his then elastic step by sweeping strides to the front of his party, and enabled him to largely contribute to the molding of those sentiments and influences which precipitated our late civil conflict, but seemed to want the energy demanded at the time for a more vigorous prosecution of the war. It so happened, in the winter of 1863, soon after Horatio Seymour had been elected Governor of this State on the issue of a more vigorous prosecution of the war, that a judge of the Supreme Court for the northern district, where I was born and reared to manhood, invited me to accompany him on a visit to Albany. His political biases were decidedly Republican — mine were as decidedly Democratic ; but as we were equally patriotic in an ardent desire to put down the rebellion, he did not hesitate to introduce me to his Republican friends, among whom was a noted Republican partisan, who, honored and re-

spected, has passed into the political history of
the State as one of its Senators and prominent
Republican leaders, greatly persuasive in the
councils of the party at the time. I refer to
Senator Ben Field. After some conversation
it was arranged that they should call on Judge
Low, who then, as lately, was the sitting Senator
from the Orange and Sullivan district, and I was
invited to go with them. We found Judge Low
in his apartments at the Delavan House, and
very shortly he remarked that he had been pre-
paring an address as chairman of the Republican
State Committee to the people of the State, and
invited us to hear it read. It was a powerful
appeal to the patriotism of our citizens to sustain
the war by upholding the Republican party. I
was impressed by the strength of its incisive and
unadorned statement of the remedies it proposed
for the appalling disasters that had in swift suc-
cession befallen the Union armies — our reverse at
Stone river had just astounded the country. I will
not speak further of the address than to say
that it was shortly afterward promulgated as a
party manifesto and was hailed, not only in this
State, but in all the loyal States, as the manifesto of the Republican party. It became an
accepted model of similar addresses of the party
everywhere ; platforms of conventions were built

on it, and legislation in all the loyal States, as to
providing for the vote of the Union soldier in the
field which its author carried through our Legislature, was stimulated, if not suggested, by it.
There was something more than mere suggestion of remedies that could be put on the statute
book in that document. It called for a more
vigorous prosecution of the war by the agency
of moral sentiment—the sword of the spirit of
the Union cause, so to speak, such as Cromwell and
Milton evoked in the Covenanters who fought at
Marston Moor. It was conceived to show that
the form of patriotism then conspicuous in the
Lincoln and Seward Republicanism and the
Horatio Seymour war Democracy, which aimed
only to save the Union for itself alone, with or
without slavery, could not give a more vigorous
prosecution of the war; that death to slavery as
the ruling purpose of every Union soldier and
statesman, could alone make Union armies vic-
torious and save the nation. I have often marveled at the results wrought, as I firmly believe,
by that address. It overthrew the Seward and
Weed leadership of the Republican party in this
State and transferred it to Governor Fenton.
It menaced the renomination of Lincoln at Balti-
more in 1864. It resulted in the recoil which
happens often in the law which compels ex-

In Memoriam.

tremes to meet. By success becoming too successful, it gave Horace Greeley the nomination
and support of the Democratic party for the
presidency in 1872. I have always regarded
HENRY R. Low as the primal author of these
things The lines of his political life are broadly
delineated in the address and are the logic of it.
He was chairman of the Republican State Committee when it was issued. He thereupon became the leader of our State Senate, which was
then almost unanimously Republican, though
Charles James Folger was his colleague, and
other master-minds were there; and that leadership was neither lost or impaired while he sat
in the Senate. He was an oracle on all debated
questions. His influence was considered equally
persuasive in the Assembly and Executive chamber. No suggestion of prostitution of this enor-
mous influence to private gain or advantage was
ever whispered. The Weed dynasty was over-
thrown and Fenton became Governor in 1864.
Judge Low was his most trusted adviser. The
Chase movement to either prevent the renomination of Lincoln in 1864 or compel him to a
change of policy indicated in Judge Low's address, was indorsed by nearly every Republican
member of the Legislature of this State in the
session of that year in a formal document drawn

19

and circulated by him, which was published by the New York *Tribune*, with vigorous support- ing editorials, in leaded type, from the master- pen of Horace Greeley. This document was widely circulated and became a potent factor in shaping the platform and party pledges de- manded from President Lincoln, and a different nomination by the Republican party as a condi- tion of his nomination by the Republican party. Judge Low's first period of continuous service in the Senate embraced three terms, covering the years extending from 1862 to 1868. Those were the most eventful years in the history of our State and nation, and he was during them all the unquestioned leader of the Senate of this great commonwealth. On her stalwart arm the republic leaned and to her the eyes of the nation were turned. There was no doubt of her patriotic impulses, no fear of her fealty. But there was apprehension that corruption in the ad- ministration of her local governments ; city and county would sap her generous life and weaken her potent arm ; that the accumulation of wealth and the development of resources would not keep pace with ,improvident and criminal ex- penditures, which at once impoverish and cor- rupt a commonwealth. The grandest political States are most exposed to these dangers. This

Judge Low appreciated more keenly than any
man I ever met, and his views came to be well-
known during this first period of his service in
the Senate. He also appreciated that the point
of greatest danger lay in local administration,
whether in hamlet, village, city or county. He
saw the multitude of cities in our State lifting up
their municipal crowns in rivalry and pride, and
among the great cities of Brooklyn and New
York, whose vast and growing importance he
comprehended. At that time the doctrine of
local self-government for cities had but few ad-
vocates, and the Legislature was relied upon to
govern them by special enactments on every sub-
ject affecting them. The city of New York was
not permitted to expend a dollar for any purpose
of municipal administration or improvement
without an act of the Legislature specially author-
izing it. All street railroads were authorized
and built by special charter, without the con-
sent of the city or its property owners. All
plans for rapid transit or, as it was then called,
for the relief of Broadway, were discussed and
disposed of in the Legislature. It is easy to
see that party leadership in the Legislature,
under these conditions and in those times called
upon the dominant party, as the responsible
authority, for its ablest and worthiest friend,

and it was abundantly supplied in Judge Low, in whose intelligence, talents, industry, tact, urbanity, patience, readiness in debate, practical business intuitions, local training, judicial experience, and, above all, his acknowledged integrity, formed a combination of qualities that commended him to the confidence, not only of the Senate, that he wielded in unchecked mastery, but the people of the State whom he delighted to serve—a confidence that continued and strengthened to the end of the first period of his senatorial service. The second period of his service in the Senate began after an interval of nineteen years, commencing in 1884, with the terms of nearly a majority of the present Senate, and ended a few days prior to the opening of our present session, while we were fondly hoping that the disease that pursued him to his grave would spare him to us for counsel and guidance out of his ripe experience and judgment, and for his genial and instructive companionship. No adequate estimate can be made of the usefulness, worth and powers of this remarkable man, unless the work he accomplished during the nineteen years that elapsed between his withdrawal from the Senate and his return to it be reckoned at value. I contemplate it now, since his spirit has ascended to the stars, as one

might think of an effulgent orb that has made
its flight through space on the circuit of its assigned movement, and, having accomplished the
grand purpose that set it in motion during the
time fixed for its periodicity, falls back to
the center from which it sprung and to which
it brings brighter dyes of light and more genial
rays of heat gathered from the starry fields it
has traversed. Contemplated from a practical
standpoint, we, who are proud of Judge Low and
his work, may ask with confidence, what was
this work he did? Why, he went forth into the
fields, found one blade of grass and conjured so
that two grew there; one stalk of grain and ten
others came; a back lot, and it became a garden;
a tumble-down farm-house, and it was trans-
formed into a mansion; a deserted village, and
it was peopled with prosperous denizens; an
ignorant rustic, and self-worthiness set his soul
aglow with all the fires of manly pride and ambition; forests, and they gave place to fields of
grain; streams lulling to the enchantment of echo
and solitude, and awoke them to the music of
machinery; cattle and other animals domesti-
cated to the use of man, but worthless as gold
hidden in a napkin, and they gave profit beyond
the exactions of usury. This is the character of
the work he was engaged in during those nine-

teen years. He did it by railroad building. Not as a contractor, who merely pursues the business for gain; not as a projector. who contrives a dazzling scheme for the profit of his financial manipulation, but for the intrinsic use and value of the roads themselves to mankind. He gloried in the fruits of that species of enterprise. He believed, with Lord Macaulay that "of all of the inventions, the alphabet and the printing press alone excepted, those inventions which bridge distance have done the most for the civilization of our species. Every improvement of the means of locomotion benefits man morally and intellectually, as well as materially." Inspired with this motive, he was the immediate instrumentality of building of over one thousand miles of railway and these he built expressly to develop the regions through which they projected, and which, when developed, would yield the richest harvest of benefits to the public. He saw that the Central and Erie railways lay sixty to one hundred miles apart, the former trending on the northern, and the latter on the southern, boundaries of our State, and between them there is a fertile and desirable section without means of communication with the other portions of the State. From New York to Lake Ontario he projected the Midland railroad and built it. It is now known by another

name and proved a disastrous business adventure
to him. But it has more than accomplished the
most sanguine anticipations expected from it.
Its metals now form the important connecting
link with Vancouver's island, on the coast of the
Pacific, with Manhattan island, in the harbor of
New York. This work done, he projected a
trunk line of road from Toledo to St. Louis and
chiefly built it. That, too, bears another name
than its creator gave it, but it forms now a
necessary link in the railway system that con-
nects Halifax with New Orleans. Many other
railroads were projected and brought to comple-
tion by his indomitable energy and unwearied
patience. A distinguishing feature of his railroad enterprises was the single purpose of de-
veloping the resources of the regions through
which they were constructed, and that the money
for their construction was largely supplied by
local subscriptions obtained on his personal solic-
itation. It is bewildering to think of his enor-
mous and varied labors and of the discouragements
he must have encountered; but the roads were
built and he entered upon the second period of
his senatorial service. He returned to public life
as he had nineteen years previously withdrawn
from it, with an experience and reputation, and
was at once accorded the respect and confi-

dence of his colleagues and the people of the
State, and with his great abilities not only un-
impaired but enriched with vast and varied infor-
mation derived from acquaintance, by personal
experience and observation, with every pursuit
and interest that engages or concerns society.
It may be safely said that no Senator ever sat
in the Senate who was more adequately equipped
for the discharge of the duties of the office.
His business enterprises had brought him into
contact with the agricultural, laboring, financial,
manufacturing and commercial interests of this
and many other States, and with the needs of
all localities. This was at once recognized and
though he was not accorded the nominal leadership of the Senate during his first term by his
party, yet he exerted a commanding influence in
its deliberations on all important questions. I
will not specify the great measures he advocated
or opposed — many of them are pending in some
form or another, and there may arise a difference of views respecting them at this session,
among ourselves, and it would therefore be in-
delicate to refer to his position on them ; but it
is entirely proper to say that in him our agricultural interests have lost a champion and friend
who defended them with a vigilance, intelligence
and power difficult to supply. The question of

city transit for our great metropolis has sore
need of his guiding hand. Corruption in the administration of municipal government may rejoice
at the loss of an unrelenting and dangerous foe.
Monopolies that oppress and extort from the
people, too, may rejoice, not that he was a chronic
mouser for corruption as a suspicious pessimist
who believes that villany is ever lurking in positions of responsibility and power. That was not
the character of his noble mind and heart. He
was an optimist, a believer in progress, a wel-
comer of all who brought to his notice plans for
the comfort, convenience and moral, material and
mental elevation of his fellowmen. His choice
would be to assuage a sorrow or promote a
measure of progress rather than to cast stones
at those who err. He believed that government
was established to advance society rather than
to frame Draconian codes of punishment or the
contrivances of a detective office. All those who
have plans of public beneficence and private
charity and progressive ideas, which need the
vote and advocacy of a legislator greatly in sympathy with them in whatever form or by whom-
soever presented, have lost in him their foremost
champion, counselor and friend. And, Mr. President and fellow-senators, all of us share in the
universal bereavement the loss of this great,

good, useful, wise and gentle colleague, has brought upon the Senate and the people of this State.

Senator WALKER spoke as follows :

Mr. PRESIDENT : With profound sorrow and with true sincerity, I join in paying the last official tribute of respect and friendship to the memory of our friend and colleague, HENRY R. Low. In paying this tribute, I have no desire to cover the dead with unmerited eulogy, and would not pronounce about a man so sincere as he, a word of praise in which there is the least coloring of insincerity. During the eleven years of which he was a member of this body, I have known him but a little more than three. In these three years of legislative life, associating with him from day to day, and working with him in the committee room, I have been enabled to form, what I believe to be a just estimate of his character and worth.

And now, as I turn my attention to this life so lately ended here and begun above, the words that involuntarily spring to my mind are those of Cardinal Wolsey in his advice to Cromwell — " Be just and fear not; let all the ends thou aim'st at be thy country's, thy God's, and truth's ; then if thou fall'st, O, Cromwell, thou

28

fall'st a blessed martyr." If we are to judge by
results, no more fitting or appropriate words
could our friend have taken as the motto and
inspiration of his life. The principles of justice
and courage, though not paradoxical, are not often
as happily blended in the same individual. In this
respect his life was an exception to the general
rule — quiet and unostentatious in manner, always
courteous in bearing and respectful of the opinions
of others — he at the same time had clear and well-
defined opinions of his own, and his convictions
often blazed forth in such a manner as to command
the respect and admiration of even his opponents.

As a legislator he was remarkably intelligent, tireless in industry, and generously just,
always laboring to promote that legislation which
would conduce to the prosperity of the State at
large, and the peace, comfort and well-being of
all classes and conditions of men. Without
speaking disparagingly, by way of contrast, of
the motives or ability of other members of our
honorable body, I think I may say, without fear
of contradiction, that he was preëminently the
friend of the agriculturists and farmers of the
State. It was this trait, as I observed it in his
character, which first called forth my respect
and admiration. When we consider the large
number of this class scattered throughout the

length and breadth of our State, their general intelligence, their diversified interests, the modesty of their demands, and the want of organization through which their influence is felt, when we consider all this, it is an honor worthy the highest ambition to be regarded by them as their acknowledged leader, champion and friend.

> "In halls of State he stood for many years,
> Like fabled knight, his visage all aglow,
> Receiving, giving sternly, blow for blow ;
> Champion of right."

As a faithful, industrious and painstaking legislator, Senator Low was an example well worthy of our imitation. During a part of the last session while he was with us, whether walking quietly about the Senate chamber, or sitting in his seat, we have observed the frail hold which he appeared to have upon life, and feared that in addition to the burden of years, he was bearing the heavier burden of disease. In all this he was faithful in the discharge of all his duties, and had a pleasant smile and a kind word for all who in anyway were associated with him.

As a gentleman and man of business he was honored and respected wherever he was known. For truth, integrity and honor marked all his dealings. In this the Senate of the State of New

York he was the recipient of the highest honor
it is in our power to bestow, that of President
pro tempore. In his home, where he was identified
with so many business enterprises and projects
that tend to the growth and prosperity of his
city, he was alike the kind friend and the distinguished citizen, and when the last day came,
and the places there of responsibility and trust,
which had known him so long were to know
him no more forever, as an evidence of the high
regard in which he was held, all places of business were closed as he was carried to the
church, where the old and the young, the rich
and the poor assembled to pay their last tribute
of respect, before he was laid away in his last
resting-place.

His life, which was gentle and patient, full of
work and crowned with success, is ended and
he has gone to his reward.

The year 1888, so lately closed, has been an
eventful one in the annals of our State and
nation. Many of the noblest and best have fallen
like the leaves of autumn to the earth, and by
their influence, example and achievements, enrich
it and make it better for coming generations. A
remnant of life, be it long or short, still remains
to each of us. It may not be possible for us to
move in the exalted orbits of many of those who

have preceded us, or even to reflect the luster of their brilliant achievements, but it is possible for each of us to move grandly true in his own orbit; to be the conscious possessor of a noble nature, and by diligent adherence to principle and duty be numbered among those who are faithful in that which is least.

Mr. President, as we are assembled at this time in respectful recognition of the worth and services of our departed colleague, I desire to add, to the eloquent and befitting testimonials that are here presented, this simple but sincere tribute to the memory of my friend.

Senator LANGBEIN spoke as follows:

Mr. PRESIDENT: I arise from my chair with melancholy pleasure to give my humble tribute to the memory of our departed statesman.

He was an able politician. I do not mean he was a politician in the ordinary acceptation of that word, but in its higher and true meaning. What is politics? It is the science of government. By science is meant a system of a branch of knowledge comprehending its doctrine, reason and theory. What is government? It is the exercise of authority, or direction, and restraint exercised over the actions of men. Science of government signifies that form of fundamental rules by which a nation or State is governed, or by which the members of a body politic are to regulate their social actions. It means the administration of public affairs according to established constitutions, laws and usages. In this sense the deceased Senator was an able politician.

He was a statesman, for he was a man versed in the arts of government ; especially was he a man eminent for political abilities.

Besides all this, he was a very experienced legislator. He served as a Senator in the Senate of this State during our late civil war, in the years 1862, 1863, 1865, 1866 and 1867. From the year 1867 to the year 1884 he was not a Senator, but in the year 1884 he reappeared in the Senate Chamber of our State, representing the Thirteenth Senate District until the day of his death.

He was a fearless investigator. I remember the time, now about three years ago, in the year 1886, when, as chairman of the Senate Railroad Committee, he was engaged in the city of New York investigating the Broadway Railway scandal. He was tireless and fearless in that investigation, and it was mainly due to him, assisted by the invaluable aid of that learned and accomplished departed Republican statesman, Roscoe Conkling, that one of the most stupendous frauds of our age was unearthed, and many of the perpetrators were punished.

During all these years of his political career he was free from even a taint of suspicion of collusion or corruption.

In the last year of his life he must have suffered greatly. Several times I have seen his sad face, as he sat in his chair, with his head bowed down, pained with physical disability, and anxious about the welfare of our State, which he loved so well.

He was true to the people; he was true to his party.

It is by no means a fact that death is the worst of all evils; when it comes it is an alleviation to mortals who are worn out with sufferings.

We may say of our deceased friend:

"Though old, he still retain'd
His manly sense and energy of mind.
Virtuous and wise he was, but not severe;
He still remembered that he once was young:
His easy presence check'd no decent joy.
Him even the dissolute admir'd; for he
A graceful looseness when he pleased put on,
And laughing could instruct."

He was kindness itself. A more genial, kindly nature for an old gentleman I never knew, and it was as unostentatious as it was kind. Whoever knew him, he must be long remembered by

> "That best portion of a good man's life,
> His little nameless, unrecorded acts
> Of kindness and of love."

Senator COGGESHALL spoke as follows:

Mr. PRESIDENT: It was my privilege to enjoy the acquaintance and friendship of Senator Low. I admired him living and mourn him dead. With chastened heart, and tender, reverent memory, I offer my humble tribute to his greatness and worth.

We turn instinctively to-day to the vacant seat he occupied; we recall the benevolent face, the kind manner, the uniform courtesy, which were always his. We can not realize that this familiar presence is forever gone from our midst; that we may never again meet and greet him.

But the unoccupied chair, the unanswered roll-call, his continued absence, confirms the sad intelligence that he is dead. He has gone to a rich and ripe reward, where loftiness of soul and honesty of intention are most fully appreciated.

His was an accomplished life. A life devoted
to usefulness, rewarded by success and crowned
with honor. We may grieve at his "taking off,"
but we are not permitted to complain. To complain at the close of such a life is to complain
that the ripened fruit drops from the overloaded
bough, that the golden harvest bends to the sickle,
that the purple twilight succeeds the perfect day.
For such a life Eloquence shall lift her impassioned
voice and Poetry shall sing her sweetest lays.

For such a man praise, honor, imitation; but
not tears! Tears for him who has failed; tears
for him who, wearied with the march of life,
"by the wayside fell and perished;" not for
him who finished the journey.

We lament, therefore, in no complaining spirit
for Henry R. Low. With our regret that he
has died is mingled our thankfulness that he
has lived. The city in which he dwelt so long,
and in whose prosperity and development he was
so deeply interested, the district and the State
that he served so faithfully and so well, may
appropriately inscribe his name on the roll of
their honored dead.

The Senate, which he informed with wise
counsels, which he adorned with dignity of manner and purity of life, bears equal testimony to
his abilities and to his integrity.

In Memoriam.

We honor his memory. We appreciate his services. We deplore our loss.

Of him it may truthfully be said: "They who knew him best loved him most."

He had a genial, sunny disposition; a warm, sympathetic heart; and "he wore the radiance of his soul in his face." In social life he was always the same open-handed, large-hearted, generous, pleasant friend; treating all who came within the circle of his influence, rich or poor, exalted or lowly, with the same rare, exquisite courtesy. Contact with the world, its jostlings and collisions, had no effect to mar the simplicity of his character or cool the warmth of his heart. That retained a freshness almost boyish. Though advanced years and feebleness of health invited him to repose, though he had climbed the rugged pathway of life far up the Alpine heights, so that the glistening peak was near at hand and winter's snow all around him, he looked down upon the valleys below, glowing with tropical gorgeousness, and sympathized with the joyousness of earth's youth, the laughter of children, the music of birds, the joy and hope and universal gladness, without envy or sigh that he could not descend, but must hold on his way until the bleak summit was reached.

He could well have claimed that he had done his full share of public duty, but the habits of a life of active usefulness would not permit him to do this.

From the early morning of life, all through its meridian and afternoon, he had been a faithful worker. Industry and energy, hopefulness and enthusiasm, were his essential characteristics.

Though naturally frail in body he was vigorous and persistent in both physical and mental action, and his life and achievements attest the possibilities and opportunities which cluster about American citizenship.

He was an earnest and successful student of books, of men and affairs.

He developed a fair fortune for himself, and he gave most liberally of his possessions, his strength, his abilities and his time to the improvement of his fellow-men, to the growth and prosperity of the community, and to the stability and perpetuity of the State.

Having acquired a fortune, he suffered, as many do in these changing times, a loss of his estate. But he was undaunted in the face of disastrous failure; and with that cheerful courage which characterized him he launched into new enterprises and speedily regained the financial resources for usefulness which had been swept

away. In the hour of failure he was neither
dismayed nor cast down, and in the hour
of financial success he exhibited no unreason-
able pride. His desire to acquire wealth was
coupled with a still stronger desire to use his
acquisitions for the benefit of those around
him.

Senator Low was not only a kind friend and
an enterprising, public-spirited citizen, but he
was also an able representative.

Called repeatedly to positions of public trust
and responsibility, he faithfully discharged every
known obligation.

His legislative career was marked by the most
conscientious discharge of duty, by the most
patient attention to every detail of legislation,
and by the advocacy of laws for the promotion
and protection of the great agricultural interests
of the State. He was an earnest, faithful,
devoted champion of the people's rights. The
sincerity of his devotion to duty was the charm
of his success. He was prudent, sagacious,
laborious, wise. He was a brave, cautious, vigi-
lant pilot, never departing from his chart or
neglecting his compass.

He was a sentinel who never left the post of
duty. His positions were thoughtfully taken,
securely fortified and persistently defended.

What he said he considered well, and he had that rare wisdom which is born of steady judgment, mature experience, intelligent conscience and generous impulse. There was with him always a wise and a considerate propriety of conduct, a love of truth, an unaffected modesty, a benevolent and kindly charity, which was both a principle and rule of his life.

Earnest in the discharge of his duties he was never obtrusive, never presumptuous nor impulsive, and he never said a word calculated to inflict a wound or injure the feelings of the most sensitive.

Uncomplainingly he bore the burden of disease. The condition of physical health in which he performed his duties here saddened us all; yet complaint never escaped his lips, and he would force his weak body to its work with a vigor and courage that it is not extravagant to call heroic.

As I think of him thus resolutely and cheerfully struggling against the infirmities with which he contended, as I remember his simple, unostentatious life, the words of the poet seem as though dedicated to him, and as if expressive of his thoughts had he but uttered them:

> "I am weary of my burden
> And fain would rest."

In Memoriam.

Every leaf upon life's shore lines
 Is a gem;
Not a withered one is drooping,
While the hand of love is looping
And into garlands grouping
 All of them.

Not a storm cloud gathers
 On the air;
Only summer clouds are drifting,
And the summer breezes sifting,
And sweetest perfumes lifting
 From gardens fair.

Only music soft and melting
 Soothes the soul;
And its billows mild and wooing,
With a gentle hand undoing
All the cares that were bestrewing
 Each earthly goal.

I will take my burden for a pillow
 And lie down to rest;
God's love shall dwell beside me,
And no clouds shall ever hide me
From the loving ones that guide me
 To the portals of the blest.

The duties of the dead Senator are
ended; with him the great account is closed.
Even this solemn hour, with his name on
every lip, is nothing to him. His silent, inani-
mate form is alike indifferent to censure or to
praise.

But to us, the living, this occasion is freighted with interest and admonition.

Treasuring in our hearts his memory, exemplifying in our lives his virtues, may we remember,

> "As each goes up from the field of earth,
>   Bearing the treasures of life,
> God looks for some gathered grain of good,
> From the ripe harvest that shining stood
>   But waiting the reaper's knife.
>
> "Then labor well, that in death you go
>   Not only with blossoms sweet;
> Not bent with doubt and burdened with fears
> And dead, dry husks of the wasted years,
>   But laden with golden wheat."

Senator McNAUGHTON spoke as follows :

Mr. PRESIDENT : The fact that my personal acquaintance with the deceased Senator — at his death President *pro tempore* of the Senate — began less than one year before his death, will justify me in not indulging in extended remarks on his life, character and public services, certainly, in not attempting a formal eulogy. Yet for many years I knew much of the character and value of the services rendered his constituency and the State by Senator Low ; heard him spoken of as a ripe scholar, a man of affairs, forcible and potent in deliberations touching the political questions

put in issue by his party, an upright judge, a distinguished and influential member of the Legislature, and that his name, by his party friends,
was frequently mentioned in connection with the
highest office in the gift of the people of this
State.

When, at the beginning of the previous
session of this Senate, it was my privilege to
meet him personally, I found that not a word
too much had been said in his praise ; that he
possessed in a marked degree those traits of
mind and character which always win and command respect and admiration. He was a steadfast friend ; his heart beat for humanity regardless
of station or race, whether clothed in rags or
in silken vesture. He was the earnest, true, un-
yielding friend of the wage-earner ; his voice,
his influence were ever potent in behalf of those
who earn their bread by the sweat of their brow.
In this chamber he strove not for the ideal, but
for legislation that would prove a substantial advantage and of practical value and utility. He believed in the dignity, the usefulness of mechan-
ical and agricultural pursuits, and that agriculture
was the foundation of the wealth of a nation, the
basis of enduring prosperity to the people.

While Judge Low was a strong, zealous, but
not bitter partisan, yielding no point of advantage

to his own party, for a political opponent, by
reason of personal friendship or business, or
social relations — he was honorable to his political adversaries, his contention for his party
was always on principle — he availed himself
of no trick, device or subterfuge, or an
unmanly advantage. It has, therefore, been well,
appropriately and truly said, his death is a public
loss ; one that will be felt and deplored by the
citizens of our State. In the pathetic words of
another, "his death is a recent sorrow ; his
image still lives in eyes that weep for him."

The time of his death, with reference to the
season of the year, his mental condition, public
position and achievements, is suggestive. He had
passed the hopes of spring, the promises and
pledges of summer, had heard the chant of the har-
vesters bringing their sheaves with them; had seen
the grapes purpling and rich on the vine, and the
ripened fruit bending the boughs; all this he had
looked upon with kindly and gladdened eyes, and
winter had not locked the streams nor made
barren and bleak the face of nature, when he
passed away. So his life. The promise of his
youth had been fulfilled, he had borne his share,
aye, more than his share of toil and struggle in
the summer heat of life's battle, his well-
directed efforts had yielded fruit and good,

44

proved a blessing and an aid to humanity, notably
to the poor, the struggling and the down-trodden,
and before the chill blasts of regret or disappoint-
ment had come, or biting winds of adversity had
touched or chilled him, before malice or envy
had endeavored to harm, in the full vigor of a ripe
and cultured intellect, in the possession of every
faculty, "he has gone over to the majority; has
joined the famous nations of the dead," quietly,
peacefully, gently, calmly—"death seeming rather
to have been given to him than life taken
away." Not a word said in praise of his character, his integrity, his fidelity to truth and justice, by the orator or the press but was well-
merited; no eulogy can exaggerate his worth, his
struggles to enforce what he deemed the right,
and his private life was as pure and spotless as
the snow which lies on his grave to-night. The
good he accomplished, is the "eloquent oration of
this hour." Perhaps I ought not to have occupied
any time on this occasion when so many Senators
around this circle, from long and intimate acquaintance with Senator Low, are so well
equipped to speak of him, but I should have
done injustice to the promptings of my heart, if
I had not risen in my place and uttered these
words, testifying the love, the regard and respect
which I entertained for our deceased friend.

Senator ARNOLD spoke follows :

Mr. PRESIDENT: I did not know Senator Low as
long or as well as many Senators who have already
spoken so eloquently and truthfully in his honor,
but I knew him long enough and well enough to
have recognized and admired in him many great
and gracious qualities wiht which he was so generously endowed. In many respects Senator Low
always appeared to me to be a great man. In no
respect did he ever appear to be an ordinary
man. He had all the characteristics more or less
developed, which men attribute to those who are
called the great of the earth. He had industry,
upon which greatness in these days only is built.
He had thoughtfulness. He was full of that intellectual digestion out of which temperate and
far-seeing statesmanship grows. He was brave ;
he was honest ; he was generous and kindly disposed, and forgiving to his enemies, and above
all, Mr. President, he seemed to be gifted with
that remarkable quality which all great men
possess — the quality of faith — not that which
is said to stir the hills on their bases, but that
which is akin to it, faith in the dignity and the
fidelity, and the truthfulness of his kind. In a
word, he appeared always to be the most credu-
lous of men. Whoever had his confidence had it
all ; and this gift, shining out as it did among his

great talents, seemed to be one of the most
charming qualities of this remarkable man. He
was an old man; or at least he was approach-
ing rapidly that period which, by common con-
sent, is fixed as the limit of human life. He
had seen illustrated many times in his own experience the truth of the homely line —

"False are the men of high degree."

He knew how fickle and changeable public
sentiment is, even in the best informed com-
munities. And yet this man, with faith sublime,
would trust in the honor and fidelity of human
nature, and he trusted it because he lived in and
breathed that atmosphere.

There was another charming quality which
Senator Low seemed to possess to a remarkable degree, and that was, he always seemed to
be a young man. He had a body tortured by
pain and tried by disease. He had seen mis-
fortunes; he was, indeed, like one of old, "ac-
quainted with grief;" and yet time had not
embittered his temper nor had sorrow soured his
disposition. He seemed to have caught in early
youth of the color of the morning "incense
breathing morn," and to have brought him the
graces of early life, emblems of beauty and
hope which adorn early manhood, and he seemed
to have set them on the declining slope of old

47

age that they might light his pathway to the tomb.

Mr. President, if there is any test, I do not know of any that is more accurate than this, by which we may judge of the success of any man's life; it is, how much of the purity, the simplicity, the tenderness and generosity of early youth, he brings with him into old age. He who succeeds in this, as did Senator Low, has indeed discovered what that adventurous Spaniard searched for in vain, the fountain of perpetual youth.

I must criticize, Mr. President, one word used by one Senator in these charming services; it is the word "late" as applied to our departed friend. My faith teaches me that the friendship that he inspired is quick with life eternal. That when the stars above us grow pale with age, "and are to dumb forgetfulness a prey," the thought that binds my friend and me, will still shine in the firmament of God's beatitudes forever.

Mr. President, whoever has thoughtfully observed these services will have noticed a golden thread running through every discourse. The Senator from the twenty-first (Sloan) put his own just and accurate estimate upon the character of our distinguished friend; but he spoke too of his firm and steadfast friendship; and the

Senator from the Second (Pierce) so tenderly —
true to his nature — set forth his charming qualities, his abilities and his patriotic fidelity; and
yet to his pure, firm and enduring friendship he
gave the highest meed of praise; and so it went
through every speech. Friendship is the golden
thread, it seems, on which we all unite and
which joins us to the man departed.

I am reminded by this, Mr. President, of a
fable designed to illustrate the eternity and
nobility of friendship. The noblest sentiment
and the purest that grows out of human acquaintance is friendship. Like a plant of noble
origin it grows only to perfection in noble and
generous natures; it is constant in every vicissi-
tude of fortune, and, as we see so happily illustrated here, it survives the shock of that fatal
hour when we bid adieu to earth. The fable
ran this way: It was the story of five friends
who took a journey together, a long and peril-
ous journey into a distant and unknown land.
Each was gifted with tastes and qualities pe-
culiar to himself, and yet they pursued every
enterprise; they endured every privation; they
enjoyed every success as men of one mind; and
in the very hour of danger and in the forefront
of battle the noblest and the bravest of them
all came to his journey's end; and they buried

him there in the wilderness. As his friends sat
around at night, as was the custom of their
country, speaking of his great and noble nature,
each attributed to him different qualities — qualities predominant in the nature of each, as the
taste of each was different from the others. Yet
they all agreed on one thing, that he was the
purest and most faithful of friends. That in that
great household he was the noblest and eldest-
born.   There was thus one thing upon which
they could all unite, and standing around his
grave, as we do here to-night, moved by a
common impulse, they uttered this sentiment:

"Long live friendship; may the spot be ever green
    where it commenced,
And the place ever bloom where it grew,
And when all its bloom is over
And its leaves are withered and fallen
May friendship still continue."

In a certain sense, we stand around the grave
of this distinguished man to-night. His life and
his death have lessons of instruction and wisdom
for us all. There is not in the material universe
of God, the humblest living thing that does not
teach how vain that human life must be whose
ambition ends with this existence. Senator Low
died full of honors, and yet he was not satisfied;
he was a disappointed man. In the last year of

his life ambition ruled every hour. Never did
the phantom of hope lure him on and encourage
his tottering footsteps to still higher places upon
the earth more than in that last year ; and so
it continued until " life's thread, worn fine as
web of gossamer, at last gave way, and he to
the elements resigned the principles of life they
lent him."

If it were given to the dead to contemplate
and if we were permitted to hear from that distant shore the old familiar voice, in tones of
tender admonition, how impressive would its
lessons be to every ambitious man around this
circle. And yet the life and death of our friend
teaches us as though one rose from the dead :

" What shadows we are and what shadows we pursue."

Senator ROBERTSON spoke as follows :

Mr. PRESIDENT : The chair by my side has
been made vacant by death. The Senator that
filled it has passed away, and is now, I trust, in
the full enjoyment of that life which a right life
here insures.

HENRY R. LOW was born in Sullivan county,
in this State, in 1826. He came of a family somewhat distinguished and quite patriotic. One an-
cestor represented that county in the other
branch of the Legislature. Two others served

in the American army during the revolution. He
himself started out in life as a common school
teacher, the starting point of a large number of
the great men of this nation. In due time he
was admitted to the bar and won a few laurels
in his profession. Twice he was elected judge
of his native county. At length he became a
member of the State Senate. This would have
been his twelfth year of service in this body.
Here he labored to protect all the great interests
of the State. He was the champion of the
farmer and of the laborer. Here he sought to
relieve real estate of its heavy and unjust
burdens of taxation. He wanted the laborer to
receive for his labor such compensation as would
enalbe him to educate his children, support his
family and make accessible to them the comforts
and enjoyments of life. This alone will account
for his immense popularity in the Orange district. He often took part in debate here ; he
was a fluent speaker ; he stated his facts with
great clearness and force and built on them strong
and convincing arguments. It is a remarkable
fact that he seldom or never excited the envy
or jealousy of his political associates ; that he
seldom or never aroused the wrath of his political opponents. He possessed much more ability
than the average law-maker ; but his was not

a towering intellect. Had he been a great genius
he would have been less useful to his constitu-
ents, less useful to the people of the State. He
was noted for amiability, for gentleness and purity
of character, for fidelity to the interests in-
trusted to his care, for devotion to friends, and
for courteous treatment of all with whom he
came in contact. He had a laudable ambition,
and had he lived higher honors would undoubt-
edly been conferred upon him.

May we so live, may Providence so guide
us, that when we shall be called from earth our
regrets will be as few, our prospects as bright as
those of our departed associate, whose virtues
we this night commemorate.

Senator CANTOR spoke as follows:

Mr. PRESIDENT: I do not propose at this hour
to indulge in any extended eulogy on the life or
services of Judge Low. Others have spoken upon
this floor whose acquaintanceship with him extended over a greater period of time than my
own, and who, perhaps, have a stronger and
greater familiarity with the eminent services
which he has rendered to the people of his district and of the State. It was my good fortune,
as a member of the lower branch of the State
Legislature, to have witnessed during the past

three years the services which he rendered to the people of the State, in this, the upper branch. I noticed that while brilliancy was not a distinguishing characteristic of his nature or of his mental power, he had that energy, that fidelity to trust, that power of application which unfortunately, as a combination, is so rare in our public servants.

Mr. President, we differed as a minority from the political views expressed and entertained by Judge Low. We admired the many manly qualities of his nature, we appreciated his virtues, we recognized his courtesy and frankness upon all occasions, when a political contest was injected into any measures upon this floor. Widely differing from him as we did upon principles involving many public enactments, we recognized, after all, that so far as he was concerned, he was influenced by an honest judgment and a desire to perform his public services in accordance with what he believed to be the best and truest interests of the people of this State. It is for that, Mr. President, that the Democratic minority upon this floor respect, honor and revere his memory to-night. To those virtues which have been so eloquently alluded to by others, permit me to say, that those were the principles which underlay all the public actions which he per-

formed upon this floor. The principles which
influenced his conduct, and upon which he based
his official acts were those, Mr. President, which
we would have inculcated and imitated by the
rising generation and the generations that are to
follow.

> "These will resist the empire of decay
> When time is o'er and worlds have rolled away;
> Cold in the dust the perished heart may lie,
> But that which warmed it once shall never die."

Senator FASSETT spoke as follows :

Mr. PRESIDENT : The lateness of the hour ad-
monishes me, that whatever I may have to say
should be brief. These testimonials of regard,
of tender appreciation, of affection and admiration for our friend, have moved me strongly.
They are to me as they must be to all who
knew him, echoes of our own emotions — reflec-
tions of our knowledge of the man. I can not
hope to bring to the altar, I do not bring, an
elaborate and splendid garland, but my own relations to Judge Low were such that I feel, at
this time and under these circumstances, that I
would be false to myself, did I not bear public
testimony to the affection and regard in which I
held him and hold his memory. It is almost
startling, Mr. President, to reflect over what a
span that man's life extended, when measured

by man's progress. During his relations to the nation and to the State nearly all the great material forces, distinctively modern, have been invented, developed and applied. The world has experienced its most astonishing era in the rapidity of its material progress, in whatever directions these go to make up human life and human interest. Judge Low was one of the men of a generation that we regret to see is passing away, which brought about all these marvelous changes in the history of society. Think what a chasm separates us to-day in our material, our intellectual and our political history, in this country alone, from the time when Judge Low first entered public life, and yet the creation of States, of fortunes, of great cities and marvelous enterprises, witnessed in the last sixty years, have been all brought about by the devotion, the integrity, the enterprise, the industry of just such typical Americans as the friend we mourn to-night. Men die and their individual memories may fade away, but the forces they originate during life endure forever and constitute their indestructible monuments. It is an appalling thought to me, Mr. President, and fraught with many a lesson, to reflect that every act and every deed of a man continues its impulses and its influences forever, and that the great book of account is never and can never be closed until heaven and earth have rolled away like a scroll.

Into every fabric of this State and of the nation, as has been testified to by those who know his personal history well, has been in-wrought the fabric of the life of our dead friend. He was, as has been said, perhaps not a great man. Greatness comes to but few men in the history of the world, but he was a valuable man. He had about him that which I admire most of all; he was a manly man; he was a brave and fair man; a man with the courage of his convictions; a man who knew how to think and dared to act; he was of the men who constitute the strength of our nation. It is on the shoulders of such men that the stability of our institutions rest; it is from the hearts and minds and lives of such men, that our great institutions have derived their most useful characteristics, and derived the guarantee of their solidity and perpetuity. That State is richest, Mr. President, that has in its treasury the most memories of such men as he. Mr. President, that life is not successful which is occupied with the accumulation of wealth, with the acquisition of power, or the social influence, or the mere bestowment of great charities. He only is successful who,

by his life in the world, does something to make
some one somewhat better and happier for
having lived. Tested by that touchstone we all
know that the life of our friend was eminently
successful; for all the long path of his life has
been strewn those little unrecorded acts and
words of love and kindness which endear man
to his fellows. Measured by that line the life of
our friend was successful. And yet it happened
to him to reap as bountifully of the rewards of
fame as happens to most men.

Viewed from the standpoint of eternity there
is not much difference in men's lives. It matters
not whether a man be cut down at twenty, in
the flower of youth; at forty, in the full vigor of
middle-age, or falls to sleep at sixty. Measured
from the distance of eternity, that life only is
long which answers life's great end, and that
is, by helping to lift the world a little higher
and leading fellow-men a little nearer to each
other.

What more then, Mr. President, could a man
ask than that it might truthfully be said of him,
when he has passed away, not that he was a
great man, but that he lived upon the earth a
life long and successful.

The life is more than breath and the quick
round of blood; it is a great spirit and a busy

heart. We count time by heart throbs, not by figures on a dial. He lives most who feels the most, thinks the noblest and acts the best for God and fellow-man.

Senator VEDDER spoke as follows :

Mr. PRESIDENT : I am deeply moved by the proceedings of this hour. Not often, if ever, have more heartfelt, eloquent words fallen from the lips of men, and yet, how useless, after all, words are, to fully express either a deep love or a great sorrow. At such a time as this only the heart can speak, and its language are sighs and tears. Those flowers on yonder desk are more eloquent than human utterances. The vacant chair is the orator who speaks to us to-night. On the 23d day of September, 1826, at Fallsburgh, Sullivan county, N. Y., Senator Low was born. His early youth was passed working on a farm He then read law, was in due time admitted to the bar and in 1856 was elected county judge and surrogate. Before the end of his term as judge, he was elected to the Senate of this State and served three terms during the war period. Born in poverty, working on a farm, schooling himself in the winter with the earnings of the summer, were the splendid preparation and magnificent equipment by which he climbed the rugged steps

which lead to the cloudless heights of fame.
The pleasing task of tracing instance by instance
the gathering forces by which his conquests over
measures and the faith of men were won, is for
the historian rather than the eulogist, and I will
speak only of those things which all his associates saw and all his acquaintances knew. As
a Senator, during the dark days of the war, no
man from that high ground did more than he
to keep New York, not only in the orbit, but in
the van of patriotic States. To his contempo-
raries he was as a "pillar of cloud by day and a
pillar of fire by night," by which the good ship
our Father launched was guided over the sea of
trouble to the shores of peace. He was not
supremely great in any one distinguishing characteristic, but there was such a blending and har-
mony of every noble faculty that men wondered,
not so much at any one of his grand traits as they
marveled at the greatness and completeness of
them all. He bore his faculties so meek, was
so clear in his office as Senator, and was so for-
tressed with truth and right, that all the shafts
of political criticism fell broken and hurtless at
his feet. As an orator he was neither vehement
nor painfully aggressive, but was, after all, singu-
larly effective. He did not speak often, but when
he did speak he spoke with the fervor of

honesty, the persuasiveness of knowledge and the eloquence of truth. He had the ability of patience, the talent of indomitable will and the genius of hard work. He loved to labor and he knew how to wait. He had ambition, it is true, but it was not of the vaulting kind; he raised himself by lifting others. His ambition was to lay deep and broad the foundation of States upon the corner-stones of liberty, equality and justice, to "scatter plenty o'er a smiling land" and to read a people's joy in a people's eyes. His integrity was as Tineriffe in the ocean, conspicuous and against which the waves of wrong dashed and broke. "It was solid as the earth beneath, pure as the stars above." He was heroic and yielded to nothing but his conscience. He was also gentle; his manly soul loved the voice of the winter's storm and yet his kindly nature was responsive to the gentle whispering of a calm summer's evening. The horizon of his soul was enlarged by the visions he saw from his native mountain peaks and his spirit was refined by the songs of the morning and the daisies by the country roadside. But he has gone! He has traveled the pathway which leads to the stars. Grandly as he lived and as nobly and without fear he passed through the dark gates of death and entered into the endless sunshine

of the grave. To his family and neighbors he was a favorite flower cut down in the garden of domestic love. To us he has fallen as a stately oak in the stillness of the woods. Able statesman! Beloved citizen! Admirable man! Farewell.

> Weed clean his grave, you men of genius,
>   For he was your kinsman.
> Strew flowers o'er his tomb, you men of goodness,
>   For he was your brother.

The PRESIDENT put the question whether the Senate would agree to said resolutions and they were unanimously adopted by a rising vote.

Whereupon the Senate adjourned.

In Memoriam.

CONCURRENT RESOLUTION

OF THE

SENATE AND ASSEMBLY.

STATE OF NEW YORK:

IN SENATE,

February 6, 1889.

Senator COGGESHALL offered the following :

Resolved (if the Assembly concur), That there be printed for the use of the Senate, by the contractor to do the public or legislative printing, under the direction of the Clerk of the Senate, five thousand copies of the proceedings of the Senate upon the death of Hon. HENRY R. LOW, late Senator from the thirteenth district, held February 4, 1889.

STATE OF NEW YORK :
IN SENATE,
February 6, 1889.
The foregoing resolution was duly passed.
By order of the Senate.
JOHN S. KENYON,
Clerk.

STATE OF NEW YORK :
IN ASSEMBLY,
February 7, 1889.
The foregoing resolution was duly concurred in.
By order of the Assembly.
CHAS. A. CHICKERING,
Clerk.

www.ingramcontent.com/pod-product-compliance
Lightning Source LLC
Chambersburg PA
CBHW021632270326
41931CB00008B/991